animals**animals**

Deer

by **Wil Mara**

Marshall Cavendish
Benchmark
New York

Thanks to Nancy Mathews, professor of environmental studies
at the University of Wisconsin, Madison, for her expert reading of this manuscript.

Marshall Cavendish Benchmark
99 White Plains Road
Tarrytown, New York 10591-5502
www.marshallcavendish.us

Library of Congress Cataloging-in-Publication Data

Mara, Wil.
Deer / by Wil Mara.
p. cm. — (Animals animals)
Summary: "Provides comprehensive information on the anatomy, special skills,
habitats, and diet of deer"—Provided by publisher.
Includes index.
ISBN 978-0-7614-2926-5
1. Deer—Juvenile literature. I. Title. II. Series.
QL737.U55M293 2008
599.65—dc22
2007027328

Photo research by Joan Meisel

Cover photo: Malcolm Schuyl/Alamy

The photographs in this book are used by permission and through the courtesy of:
Alamy: Robert McGouey, 13; Renee Morris, 14; Wolfgang Kaehler, 18; Arco Images, 28; Peter Casolino, 36;
Jeff Greenberg, 38; Mike McEnnerney, 40. *Animals Animals - Earth Scenes*: Alan G. Nelson, 1; Peter Weimann, 25;
Gordon & Cathy Illg, 26. *Corbis*: George D. Lepp, 24; Buddy Mays, 34; Galen Rowell, 41. *drr.net*: Heidi &
Hans-Jurgen Koch, 6; Dave Welling, 16; Steve Austin, 31; Blair Seitz/Stock Connection, 33.
Minden Pictures: Tim Fitzharris, 7; Tui De Roy, 20. *Peter Arnold Inc.*: D. Hoell, 4; C. Huetter 9; S.E. Arndt 10;
Bruce Lichtenberger, 19; C. Krutz, 22; John Cancalosi, 30.

Editor: Joy Bean
Publisher: Michelle Bisson
Art Director: Anahid Hamparian
Series Designer: Adam Mietlowski

Printed in Malaysia

1 3 5 6 4 2

Contents

1 Introducing the Deer

A small herd of white-tailed deer stands in a misty meadow at sunrise. The young, still marked with spots that will disappear over time, are nibbling on fresh grass, while the adults—all female—remain alert for predators. If the deer sense danger, they will bound away with incredible speed and disappear into the surrounding woodland. For now, however, they are content to fill their bellies in the morning calm.

Deer are a diverse group of mammals that exist in a wide variety of sizes, colors, and habitats. They are known for their secretive ways, their nervous personalities, and their tremendous grace.

Unlike most deer, these sika deer will keep their spots throughout their lives.

Moose belong to the Cervidae family, which includes deer, elk, and caribou.

Deer belong to a family of mammals called *Cervidae*. Other cervids you may know include moose, elk, and caribou. The Cervidae family also includes animals with strange names like brockets, wapiti, sambars, and muntjacs. These animals share many characteristics.

There are more than thirty different species of deer in the world. Deer can be found on every continent except one—Antarctica. This is likely because they

6

could not survive the frigid temperatures and harsh environment. Deer are also rare in Africa—just one species lives there, and it is found only in a few northern forests. There were no deer in Australia until about two hundred years ago, when many species were introduced from other countries. Today, there are about a half-dozen different deer species still on that continent.

The typical deer has a sleek body, slender but powerful legs with two large toes covered by hooves.

A deer's long neck and large ears help it detect predators from far away.

Species Chart

General Characteristics

- **Length (head to body):** 6 to 7 feet (1.8 to 2.1 meters). However, the largest species, the moose, averages 7.5 to 10 feet (2.3 to 3 m), while the smallest, the pudu, averages only 2.75 to 3 feet (0.83 to 0.91 m).

- **Height (ground to shoulder):** 4 to 5 feet (1.2 to 1.5 m). Moose can reach as high as 5 to 7 feet (1.5 to 2.1 m), but the pudu is only 10 to 16 inches (25 to 41 centimeters) tall.

- **Weight:** 200 to 350 pounds (90 to 160 kilograms). The moose is the heaviest species, weighing an average of 1,250 to 1,500 pounds (567 to 680 kg), while the diminutive pudu rarely weighs more than 15 to 25 pounds (7 to 11 kg).

The pudu are the smallest deer in the world, weighing up to just 25 pounds (11 kg).

Deer can vary greatly in their coloring. These red deer have
brown fur on top and gray on their necks and bellies.

◆ **Coloration:** Mostly a shade of brown, but some can also be gray, often with reddish highlights. The belly, underside of the tail, and lower part of the neck are sometimes lighter colored than the rest of the body, often white. Some species have spotting or short striping along their bodies and on their faces, particularly when young. A few also have undersides and legs that are darker than their torsos.

◆ **Life span:** About ten years for most species, but up to twenty is not unknown.

Did You Know . . .
A male deer is often called a buck, while a female deer is known as a doe. Other names—less commonly used—include stag and bull for the males, and hind or cow for the females.

It has a long neck, and an elongated snout. Its ears are also long, and they can swivel easily, which allows them to detect sounds from different directions. The eyes are large and round and are set well apart on the head. This helps the animal stay aware of what is going on around it in all directions. The average height of a deer is about 4 to 5 feet (1.2 to 1.5 m) from ground to shoulder, and its length is about 6 to 7 feet (1.8 to 2.1 m) from the tip of its nose to its tail. The largest member of the deer family is the moose, which can grow to 7.5 feet (2.3 m) high, while the smallest deer, the little pudu, grows to only 10 to 16 inches (25 to 40 cm) high. A deer's tail is small, and it usually has light-colored fur, often white, underneath.

Most deer are a shade of brown, but they can also be so dark that they look almost black. Some deer are gray colored, and others may have reddish highlights. They can also have very light fur under-neath, covering most of the belly and running at least partway up the underside of the neck. Even with these generalizations, however, it should be noted that a deer's coloration and general appearance can vary tremendously. Some moose, for example, have very dark torsos with light-colored legs, while others have solidly dark fur from top to bottom. Some deer species have spots and even a few stripes, especially when they are younger. There is no standard deer coloration, height, or length. There is a great amount of variation.

Perhaps the most unusual characteristic of a deer's body is its *antlers*. These are branchlike horns that

A deer's antlers can grow very large and develop a layer of velvety skin on them.

Deer scrape the velvet off their antlers when it is no longer needed.

grow from the top of a deer's head. All male deer have them, as do a few females, such as caribou. A deer will begin to grow antlers by its second year of life. The antlers will reach full size within a few months. The growing antlers are covered with a layer of skin called *velvet*. Fine hairs grow from the skin, giving it a velvety look and feel. The velvet is filled with blood vessels that feed the antlers the vitamins and minerals necessary to build up the bone and to promote normal antler growth. Once the antlers have developed fully, the velvet is no longer needed. The deer will then scrape it off by rubbing its antlers against a hard surface like a rock or a tree. Deer lose their antlers each year, usually in the winter, and then grow a new set in early spring. Antlers are used in a number of ways. Antler branches have sharp tips, so the deer can use them as a weapon. The males will fight each other for females by slamming their antlers together. Males may also use the antlers to mark their territory by making cut lines in tree bark. In some Cervidae species, antlers can grow to an enormous size. In moose, for example, antlers can be as wide as 6 feet (1.8 m) across.

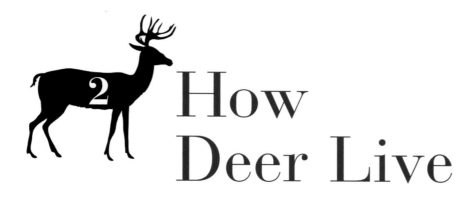

How Deer Live

Most deer do not live in one particular area for their entire lives in the way that turtles live in one pond or birds return to one nest their whole lives. Instead, they tend to roam over a large general region called a *home range*, and the males usually have a larger area than do the females. In terms of habitat, deer can be found in many different types of areas. Some live in swampland, while others live in the mountains. Most prefer the quiet of undeveloped woodlands, particularly where there is a good mixture of open spaces, trees, bushes and shrubs, and bodies of water. Deer live in these areas in order to remain close to food sources and to places where they can hide if they feel

Deer live in many parts of the world, but one thing that unites them is their need to stay close to water.

threatened. They will also take to the water from time to time, and they are excellent swimmers. In colder parts of the world, deer may move out of their normal living area during the winter to avoid the frost and snow.

Socially, deer vary tremendously. Some, like the roe deer, spend most of their lives alone. Others, such as the white-tailed deer, travel in groups of two or three. A few species form larger groups known as *herds*, and some gather in the hundreds.

Did You Know . . .

Although it is rare, some deer have been known to turn carnivorous and eat other animals. For example, deer in areas where their normal food items have been scarce have been known to feed on tiny birds and, occasionally, the meat of animals that have already died.

These swamp deer live and travel together in a herd.

Deer rest and sleep in a bed of tall grasses or weeds.

Female red deer, for example, will give birth alone but then spend the rest of their time in large congregations. Overall, female deer tend to herd more than males.

Like humans, deer are usually active during the day and sleep at night. This makes them *diurnal*. They do most of their feeding, however,

Grass, leaves, flowers, and buds are the top food choices of deer.

during the morning and evening hours, when the sun is either going up or coming down. This is when they are least likely to be attacked by *predators*—animals that hunt them. During the night, deer make their beds in tall grasses or weeds—ideal places to hide. They rarely use the same bedding spot twice.

Deer eat only plant matter, which means they are *herbivores* (as opposed to being *carnivores*—animals that feed on the flesh of other animals). They prefer to eat softer items such as grasses, flowers, buds, and young leaves. If they are hungry enough, however, deer will also eat tougher items, such as large leaves, stems, twigs, branches, and, in extreme cases, even tree bark. They eat their food quickly, so as not to be seen by predators, and they do not chew their food as much as other animals do. Instead, they swallow the partially chewed food, where it will sit in the stomach for a while and then come back up in a sticky mass called *cud*. The deer will chew the cud more thoroughly, then finally swallow it for good. Animals that eat in this way, such as cows and sheep, are called *ruminants*.

3 A Deer's Life Cycle

The life cycle of most deer begins in the fall, when males go in search of a mate. This mating period is often called a deer's *rut*. Sometimes more than one male will be interested in the same female (or herd of females), at which point some gentle fighting between the males may begin. They will snort and slap the ground, and often ram their antlers together. It is a show of strength more than anything else, for they are not truly trying to harm one another. The male displaying the greatest power gets to choose a female with which to mate.

A male deer follows after a female deer during their mating season.

This deer is pregnant and will most likely give birth to just one baby.

A doe's *gestation period* (the time it takes for the young to develop inside her body) can last anywhere from six to nine months, depending on the species and its location. She will consume as much food as possible in order to pass along sufficient nutrients to the developing embryo or embryos. Then, in spring or early summer, she will have her baby or babies—the number of newborns depends on the species. Some types of deer only have one newborn per year, while others have two. (There are Asian species that can have even more, but this is rare.)

The newborns are called *fawns*. They are born with spotted fur and spindly legs. They come into the world with their eyes open and begin walking within a few days. They are too fragile to do much else however. The mother will hide them for the first month to keep them safe from predators. The spots on their fur also protect them; lying on the ground among waving

A mother cares for her fawn.

Did You Know . . .

In some species, the does have the ability to hold off giving birth until a time of year when it would be safest for the newborns, such as when most predators have moved away or when there is plenty of food for the fawns to eat. This trait is called delayed implantation.

Young deer stay close to their mothers during their first year of life.

26

grasses, newborns often look like nothing more than a sun-dappled rock or log. If a predator does approach, the mother will either fight it off or run away from the fawns in the hope that the attacker will follow her and leave her babies alone. Male deer are not involved in the raising of the young, so they play no role in their protection.

The mother will also nourish her fawns by having them drink milk from her body. After four to six weeks, the mother will take the fawns from the nesting site and teach them to eat solid food items and to swim. They learn mostly by simply watching her. Sometimes a group of mothers will gather all their young in a herd. The fawns are eating on their own by this time, and they will play with each other as their bodies grow ever stronger. Many of the young stay with their mothers through the first year, but by the second season they move on and begin life on their own. Young males are generally ignored by older males when the new breeding cycle begins, because they are too young to mate and therefore pose no threat. A male must be about eighteen months old before it can begin mating, and a female cannot give birth until around the same time.

4 Survival in the Wild

Deer are peaceful creatures by nature. They prefer to live quietly among themselves. This makes them an easy target for predators, and there are many animals that think of deer as food. The most common predators are wild dogs and cats, including wolves, wolverines, coyotes, foxes, cougars, tigers, mountain lions, and bobcats. Deer must also be wary of carnivorous bears, large snakes (such as pythons), and even large birds. Eagles, for example, have been known to snatch small deer right off the ground.

When a deer is attacked, it has no weapons for fighting back. It does not possess sharp teeth, claws, or any type of poison. Even the males' antlers are not

The mountain lion is one of many predators that feed on deer.

When a deer feels threatened, it stands motionless to blend into its surroundings.

designed for warding off attackers. Deer simply are not built for combat. Instead, they try to avoid fights. When they are out in the open, regardless of what they are doing, deer remain alert to what is going on around them. Their hearing and eyesight are excellent, and they will pause at the first sign of trouble. This method of going still, or freezing in position, makes it tough for other animals to see them, since most deer have coloration that allows them to blend into their surroundings.

If a deer suspects danger nearby, it will take off running. If a predator leaps into view, the deer will lead the animal through the most difficult course it can find—over large rocks, through bushes, and between trees. The idea is to exhaust the attacker and force it to give up the chase. It is also hard for predators to keep pace with a deer, since many can run at

Deer have the ability to run quickly and leap great heights in order to get away from danger.

speeds of up to 40 miles (64 kilometers) per hour. Some deer also tend to bounce as they run, in a way similar to wild rabbits. This enables them to get a better look at their surroundings—the higher they jump, the more they can see. This is often crucial in figuring out where to go when being pursued by a bobcat or a wolf.

Deer must also be cautious of humans. There is little doubt that human beings are one of the deer's top predators. All across the globe, as human populations increase, the deer population (and those of other animals) continues to shrink. Every time we level a forest to build more homes or office buildings, we destroy a place for deer to live. This is called *habitat destruction*.

Humans have also been hunting deer for centuries, both for sport and for meat. Even before the first European settlers came to America, Native Americans were capturing and killing deer for meat and milk, and they were making blankets and clothing from deer skin. After European settlement, so many deer had been killed that they were completely wiped out in some areas.

Some deer have trouble finding places to live because their habitats are being destroyed to make room for stores or houses.

Did You Know . . .
Many people fear the spread of Lyme disease through the presence of deer, since the disease's main carrier is the deer tick. However, studies suggest that reducing the deer population in a given area has no affect on the number of Lyme cases that occur. In fact, in many areas where Lyme disease is common, the local deer populations are quite small.

In areas where there is a large deer population, as well as a lot of people, deer crossing signs like this one warn drivers to be on the lookout for the animals on the road.

Today, hunters have become so skilled, and their equipment so effective, that deer have little chance against them. Hunting deer does allow some benefits. In certain areas, an overabundance of deer can cause problems for the human population there. For example, too many deer can cause numerous accidents, such as when deer try to cross the road but end up in front of cars and then freeze in position. Sometimes this can cause human deaths. In addition, deer can damage environments and actually harm another animal's chance at survival by consuming too much food. There is only so much food in a given area, and if a deer population grows too large, other animals will not have enough for themselves. Also, heavy deer populations can throw the delicate balance of nature into chaos. For example, if deer eat too many of the flowering plants that bees need to produce honey, the bees will suffer. Also, with less material to build nests, certain birds may leave the area. Thus, keeping deer populations under control by allowing hunting at certain times of the year can be a good idea.

5 The Future of the Deer

It is difficult to predict what will happen to worldwide deer species in the years ahead. There is little doubt they will continue to be hunted for their meat, for their hides, and for sport. In addition, hundreds of thousands of deer are killed each year when struck by cars and trucks as they try to cross roads.

There are ways to help deer, however. When a particular deer species becomes rare, it can then be protected by an endangered-species program. This means a government can create laws making it illegal to capture, kill, or otherwise harm a member of the species. Similarly, some governments and private

This baby Pere David's deer was bred in captivity at the Bronx Zoo in New York City. This species is in danger of becoming extinct.

Another endangered deer is the Key deer. This sign warns motorists to beware of them in the Florida Keys.

Did You Know . . .
Perhaps the rarest of all deer species is Pere David's deer. It used to live in the marshlands of western and northern China, but it was slowly wiped out by hunting and habitat destruction. Today, Pere David's deer exists only in captivity, mostly in zoos.

organizations run *captive-breeding programs.* They breed endangered species in a laboratory, raise the young, and then release them into the wild. This, in turn, will gradually increase their numbers in nature and, hopefully, get them off the endangered-species list someday. Captive-breeding programs have been very successful with other animals.

There are a number of endangered deer species worldwide, including the following:

38

- Pere David's deer, *Elaphurus davidianus*—Originally found in western and northern China.

- Calamian deer, *Axis calamiansis*—Native to the Calamian Islands, which are part of the Philippines.

- Kuhl's deer, *Axis kuhlii*—Exists only on the island of Bawean, in Indonesia.

- Philippine spotted deer, *Cervus alfredi*—Native to Panay Island, in the Visayas island group of the Philippines.

- Sika deer, *Cervus nippon* (certain subspecies only)—Many subspecies, found throughout eastern Asia.

- Mesopotamian fallow deer, *Dama dama mesopotamica*—Found in small protected areas in Iran, but almost extinct in the wild.

- South Andean deer, *Hippocamelus bisulcus*—Found in mountain regions of Chile and Argentina.

Similar to the endangered-species program is the effort by many governments to protect the land that deer and other animals call home. By declaring these areas off-limits to hunters and builders, the deer are allowed to live free, threatened only by their natural predators. It is against the law for anyone to harm the wildlife in a protected area, and the penalties can be severe—steep fines and, in some cases, jail sentences.

Although humans have hunted many deer species to near *extinction* (the point at which a species no longer exists), we have also helped deer by hunting their predators. For example, widespread hunting of coyotes and wolves has allowed deer in certain areas

This sika deer is safe from hunters because it lives on protected land at the Arne Nature Reserve in England.

The replanting of forests helps many deer and other animals find places to live.

to flourish. Without these predatory animals, the deer can eat and breed freely. Sometimes this does more harm than good, however. With too many deer in one area, the food supply quickly becomes wiped out, and then the deer risk starving to death. This alone is a lesson in the delicate balance of nature—everything is related to everything else in some way.

Other efforts to protect deer include the replanting of destroyed forests—which creates new habitats for them—and the limitation of hunting season, which allows hunters to kill an unlimited number of deer, but only within a limited time frame. For example, one state might have its annual deer-hunting season for only two weeks. One advantage to hunting in this manner is that it keeps the deer population from growing too large.

Glossary

antlers—Branchlike horns that protrude from the heads of most male deer, as well as on heads of female caribou.

captive-breeding program—A program designed to breed rare species in safe, controlled conditions, usually with the intention of eventually releasing the animals into the wild.

carnivore—An animal that feeds on the flesh of other animals.

Cervidae—The scientific name for the family of animals that includes all deer species.

cud—A sticky mass of partially chewed and digested food that comes back up from the stomach to be chewed again.

diurnal—Active during the day.

extinction—No longer in existence.

fawn—A newborn deer.

gestation period—Amount of time between mating and birth; the time it takes a baby to fully develop inside its mother.

habitat destruction—The ruining of a natural area.

herbivore—An animal that feeds on plant matter, such as leaves and flowers.

herd—A group of animals that feed and move about together.

home range—The total area in which an animal lives.

predator—An animal that preys on another.

ruminant—A mammal with four legs and hoofed toes, and that chews its cud.

rut—An annually recurring period of sexual excitement and reproductive activity in male deer.

velvet—The layer of skin covering a deer's antlers; its fine hairs give it a velvety look and feel.

Find Out More

Books

Macken, JoAnn Early. *Deer.* Milwaukee, WI: Weekly Reader, 2005.

Murray, Julie. *Deer.* Edina, MN: Buddy Books, 2005.

Patent, Doroth Hinshaw. *White-tailed Deer.* Minneapolis, MN: Lerner Publications, 2005.

Sullivan, Jody. *Deer: Graceful Grazers.* Mankato, MN: Capstone Press, 2003.

Web Sites

Animal Diversity Web site on the family Cervidae
http://animaldiversity.ummz.umich.edu/site/
accounts/information/Cervidae.html

Enchanted Learning site on deer, including
many activities and drawings that can be
printed out and colored
http://www.enchantedlearning.com/subjects/
mammals/deer/

French site (in English) with information
about deer
http://cerfs.free.fr/english/english.htm

World Deer Organization, with information
on many deer species
http://www.worlddeer.org/

Index

Page numbers for illustrations are in **boldface**.

About the Author

Wil Mara is the author of more than eighty books, many of which are reference titles for young readers. More information about his work can be found at www.wilmara.com